MAKE LONELINESS

make loneliness

J. REUBEN APPELMAN

OTIS BOOKS / SEISMICITY EDITIONS

The Graduate Writing program
Otis College of Art and Design
LOS ANGELES **O** 2008

Book design and typesetting: Rebecca Chamlee

ISBN-13: 978-0-9796177-0-6
ISBN-10: 0-9796177-0-7

OTIS BOOKS / SEISMICITY EDITIONS
The Graduate Writing program
Otis College of Art and Design
9045 Lincoln Boulevard
Los Angeles, CA 90045

www.otis.edu
www.gw.otis.edu
seismicity@otis.edu

TABLE OF CONTENTS

SHAVED_33

as found by the children of One A.,
bedded by the countess,
hanged by undertow off the coast of unknown –
resurfaced as person of interest.

Letter To The Countess

There's a pain in my side and it's prurient. I am reaching toward a crowd and they won't help me. When I unbutton my clothes you will hold me by my bare waist and you will wear a head-dress and dance with me. There will be sentries who will shoot us but this will come later. I will be blind when I love you, and will receive parking tickets. This is a damp night of logic and sermons lasting thirty-three years so far. And a summit. And a flower on the summit I place behind your ear.

Culled: I will chase you for three-hundred miles through black-berry bushes and then we will be killed. You hold me by my bare waist in the village. You twirl me. My human heart beats like a throw rug. I become deaf when the sentries advance.

Letter To My Children

I wish you were lonely. You would call me if you were lonely. You would ride me into the sea, yellow birds on a whale. I would be blubber, and you air. We would be happy. All fat and nothing together, leaping toward continents. Eventually I would eat you, but I wouldn't know that yet. I wouldn't be able to say one thing is food. I wouldn't know what you are when there is nothing but sea, and distance. And chlorine and pharmaceuticals. And distance.

Culled: As birds you will be prophetic, but you won't know this as birds. There will be rumors that I am mammalian, and you will suspect this as truth.

Letter To My Children

You are blackbirds whirled in wind, and have begun to want things. You have wanted a house or mood, something to fit inside or beauty. It's a shadow of barbaric glass, a glow in the dark which hangs as planets hang above your beds, all of the moons that I could build you. You speak as planets speak, but it is not enough. You are primly propped. It's a war within our windows, something to close your eyes against. You dream of jam, you count your butchered sheep to sleep. In the half-heard condition, there are geese, and treatments, a wireless and musical future.

Culled: This is a physical lightness beginning as not. You hug your bears. You hear bombs going off.

Letter to My Children

She drew a heart in her notebook, and in the heart she wrote:
Blah. We were on the bus together. (Not together.) I followed her
home. This was a burial of the dead, and thunder-said and clues.
Something to go "clickity-clack" to before you were born. A people
or whatnot. There was a need for whatever to be crossed, and the
reaching of a trill. I was respirated and kissed, I was busyness
from hill to hill. This was swiftness, loaned on emptiness, the
traces of a lore. With my finger up her ass, I administered the
"figure-four."

Culled: The heart in her notebook comes later.

Letter To My Children

Her body was like a crime scene. I kept wanting to look at it. I kept
wanting to pierce it. With a weapon. A beautiful weapon. I kept
wanting to know her, and was breathless all the time. She was
something beautiful, and with an expiration date. She was eggs,
or she was something awkward as eggs. This after being cracked,
I mean. This after we cut out paper hats together, and mine with
a few feathers, and hers with a buckle. This after she went home
crying, and with an arrowhead in her lip. This after I drew her
face on an orange, and cut it in half.

Culled: Together we were blighted steel, a diameter in the grass amid white ash and funeral cypresses. We were lowered and prayed upon. We were thickened and popped. In the gift of twilight we would relax. We would flood as rivers flood. We would know ourselves as something other, but would not be able to recognize this.

Letter To So And So

She keeps saying she's anorexic but she really looks fat. She's big as a cow, and inside her are stomachs and inside each stomach is a blueberry pie. And lard. And I know this because when I saw her on Greenfield I was wearing x-ray specs. I had my pad of paper and wrote things down. I spoke into my ring. I followed her into the bakery, where she read the news. I made love to myself in the restroom, then ordered a coffee. When she introduced herself, I was peeling away my thumbnail. The day was breaking finally. It was swelling with last year's words. We harbored a decade and wrote novels, conscious without enchantment. There were three conditions, and one of them was to be sleepy and proud. The age demanded an image, and it was an attic.

Culled: We were circumcised from dust. We were brought to the market and weighed.

Letter To My Children

You will be magnified and accepted as false. The roughshod will be discovery, one of the accused. I have said there is a universe and will have heard it. This will sound as a crucifixion: *Tap-tappit, Tap-tappit*. It's a lithograph out there and within it your kiss, and a cottonfield, alive with work. It's an infolding, some sort of conception that's bigger than us, babes. A testimony that when fallen among thieves you are jelly. I say listen to me. I have seen it or it has ticked by, a mercy without dinner. A thing in the sheets, discovered by luminol. A shirt of flame, intolerable and fishing.

Culled: I cannot remember a thing I once read, a few friends but they are in ditties.

Letter To My Children

At home I make a drink called Yesenin's Noose. I break my neck before stirring it. This happens about three or four times a week, and then I take a bath. Balance the blow dryer on my head, and slit my wrists. When I drown, it's shocking. I'm an eyeball, and capillaries. I see things down there that others don't see. Fish or whatever. And sometimes money, brilliant gold coins laid out in a trail. I find a castle, and it's full of dead people who look like me. I'm eating soup at a long table. I'm squatting beneath a boar's head, cleaning my ass.

Culled: Sometimes I awaken, but it's a paltry sum. I cannot afford to buy you the racey-cars I promised. You will inherit my kidneys, there's a legacy in this. You will inherit my windsor knot, and cufflinks. There will be a moment when your sexuality is decided, and this has passed.

Letter To So And So

My ankles bleed and the wind tickles my genitalia. I am hooked to the wood, as they say. My mother was a Windex addict, and so I was born. The voices in my head are copulating, and they are all children with steam whistles. Some of them are tenors, and others are vomiting. I carry the hush of my lips, but it is monetary. If I lay nothing more in my life I will have laid enough. The wind says this to my genitalia. It's a sucking feeling. My semen is scattered to the earth, and from it cherry trees will blossom. Bees will thrive. I will be stung to death.

Culled: I will never have believed the voices.

Letter To The Countess

I am a clean-haired Yankee and you a vagina. There is drinking to be done. I shall roll up my trousers and prance away from you. You far swooping cunt. You earth. O unspeakable love. Hooray for science! There have been many years since the password was spoken, and through me is flatulence, a negative account. This is the geologist speaking: Grab hold of your rocks and stay put. She's a doctrine waiting for ambivalence. She will machete you in your head. I am telling you I have unscrewed the doors, and behind them is a stenographer. She hears everything. Her big arms like 2×4s, and the press release of her eyes Assault Rifle Red.

Culled: You are me in this scenario. And she is you. The I in this poem is a gentlemanly tenant. A prisoner in a moth, toward the sun.

Letter To The Countess

Disturb the universe? In a minute there is time and the voices will die and fall. I should love you but am forced to the porcelain. Attendant and pinned. You have torn open my shirt and done nothing but giggled. You win. The girl next door borrowed my child for you and this is why you are hated. But even if you were beautiful you would be christened and killed. God saves the bloody marks so that we may wear them, otherwise not.

Culled: Somewhere is a mother whose child is playing, and all day. And in this day she will turn her back, and there will be lightness and absence. A creaking of a swing will stop. There will be static on the television, and she will kick it but not know why. A world will have passed. This will happen sometimes.

Letter To So And So

My right and left arms are settlements. When you lay your head on my chest you are treading in sea salt. It's a modern crowd, and not easy to please. No guard can shut me off. I suffered and was there. It was a desert, and within that a chalkboard. They had the tiniest chairs all around. A firehose spelled out the ABCs, sending off bodies against the wall. We had become maimed and mangled and this was not the Alamo. We had received some eighteen-pound shots from a fiery gun deck. We ate applesauce and waited. Nothing ever changed except the surgeon's knife. It became duller, and eventually broke. I have heard some people did not survive.

Culled: Dear So and So, the above scenario is of great interest to me, and I would appreciate your attendance at the funeral in Fall. Yours forever, Shaved_33.

Letter To The Countess

Time is no fun. I'll wear a watch that says now. I'll wear your lips
on a chain and you'll whisper to me. You'll say I'm beautiful, and
invite me to dinner. Things will happen, but we won't know what.
Nothing will happen in the next century. Nothing will change but
Ameritech, and God and gold. On Brooklyn Ferry, a rush of hearts
and spades, some summers shimmering but captainless. It's a
panorama out there, a splintered Whit. In grapes of fire or guns,
you will transect me as windpiped, a throttle.

Culled: To be in a form, as passed. This is an instant cocksucker all over me, repeat. Come in, Supernova, Come in.

Letter

At the kitchen table are corpses, and we hear the piccolos playing. A piccolo is now in fashion and you get one free when you buy a flute. There are people who can play their lips. I have played a keyboard before and it was like playing fangs. I have tried to tell my children this but they are hanging from the trees. They are urinating. It's day and night with them. Soon I will build my boy a house in the onion patch, and he will forgive me my dense-starred flag. O my daughter, child of the universe, I command you to awaken us from this half-burned barn, this shadow over the limitless and lonesome.

Culled: O my daughter, child of the universe, I command you to awaken from this half-burned barn!

Letter To The Countess

With kings and sleep, you withdraw and are unemployed and gay. Save something dashing for the dead. I am speechless, Babe, and you are grey-headed. Which of us will be gathered to the side? And made up as beds. And slept upon. And rapt in dream. You are so dashing when you're dead, and luscious. And mealy or something. It's a mysterious fucking realm. It's a formidable trust, like the drapes on our couch and you smoking. At public bars, a violet hour when the eyes have sunk.

Culled: You're always full of train. You're an animal in the snow. Your face is red, and glowing, and blue. You have bathed in the bright hues, and hymns are sung before hands that are raised, beside bodies that have fallen. To these streets.

Letter To My Children

The countess is a replica. She's a shell of a woman and when I listen to her I hear the sea. I am her bodyguard and we met in Vera Cruz or Manhattan. Once she walked by, was transparent, and adoring. I could smell her loving me but it was like playing cops and robbers with your finger. Or with rubber bands, and Tylenol. She was lucid and sinking. She was perfect, and spreading. She was a prairie full of ghosts, and as she was the countess I protected her. Nothing has changed. I am a lovely ship in the minutia of her body, barging through it as if through glacial ice. I am breaking her apart. I am looking for a place to sink my flag in the snow.

Culled: I am claiming her as cherished. We are a separate house full of throbbings. We are liquid-free and tender. I hear nothing and it's a drooping star. A skeleton walking on water.

Letter To My Children

I gave her hyacinths a year ago. She called me hyacinth girl. We could not have children because of this, and it was a sleepy corner to live in. Mine was a dull root, and it was Goodnight Bill. By the waters of Grayling I sat down and wept, but at my back I heard a blast. She was shooting blanks at me to be funny. When lovely women folly, they are followed by weekends.

Culled: I have remembered nothing. When she pulls her long hair out of her tights, I will be sickened. My shiny teeth will flash in the dark. I will bite down on dollar bills, and give them to her. There will be diseases, and laughter. I will hold about a hundred rocks in my pocket. I will use them as fuel for my rock-around rocket.

Letter To So And So

There's a whore in Dallas I saw on Montel. She's beautiful. She works at the Chevron. And you haven't been out of the house. She'll have a baby with anyone. We should visit her.

Culled: Every time we drank she had an abortion. She said, "Let's all lean left and tell suicide jokes."

Letter To So And So

We should consider seriously that I was born. That I have become scalloped is of low-tide concern. We understand one another, or there's a God that understands the gorgeous clouds before men. We are suspended from the clouds as men. We live and bounce among the seabirds, yet fear the sea. Come, ship, flaunt me away as necessary as body. Mine is a hard one now, and built to furnish souls. Make use of me. Before crowds of men or Brooklyn, kiss me on the lips in Detroit. It's a logical story will run a hundred years in the theaters. Give me my minute in the quarter slots booth, and show me how happiness ends. Light-winged smoke, Icarian Bird, melt thy pinions upward as ash from my cigarette into ripples. Forgive us our creeds and neon, it's a cosmos and there's turbulence up there.

Culled: We bounce. We bay. We behave as nostrils and dilate. This will be called Space and Time, and that anything happened will be history.

PROFIT AND LOSS

*as an attempt at correspondence with the shareholders
in the absence of funeral rites*

I

You are distant sufferings of the passive tense,
an excerpt as lineage. There are coffee shops
in Brooklyn you take as your own, but that's a
parking lot. ← Here is where I have attempted to
say something important, believing myself. Your
father was never completed, and in subsequent
billings may also have been mailed. In moments
I looked for him, in scenarios found nothing. At
checkpoints, was questioned as earmark: What is
the precise angle of retraction in this poem? What
is pepper spray? In some back alley hour, a partial
payment?

---

projected word count: 150
actual word count: 93

I knew your father only as one of the accused.
This was an island and the countess was countess
of it. At dark hours on the beach we burned our
songs to stay alive. This was beginning. When
ships would pass we closed our eyes and hummed
against our teeth. Soon I was taken into custody,
and as endowed became a slave. This was sexu-
ality, and eventually accounting. There was fruit to
eat, and propaganda. This was ethanol. There was
bedding with a high enough thread count. This
was fetishism, and truth. I mopped away semen. I
had a credit score verging on 700. This was to be
envied, a golden age when sacrifices occurred, and
tuberculosis and staph. This was a contract of sorts,
and as your father was willing, this was cheap labor.
This was to become language, and eventually tele-
vision. This was speculation, and eventually profit.
There were few left standing, and regrettably your
father. This was to sound as a jingle. This is to say
he was shuttled off to sea. There was a moaning
from the sea. It was brought to us each evening,
and lassoed back out again.

---

projected word count: 160
actual word count: 194

3

Here is my social security number: psych. Don't touch me. Add eggs, add vanilla, something like a flour mixture cracked at the center. We are beat well. To become shredded and bite-sized, we are BHT. We are Cyclobenzaprine, a summons or something. This is sugar. This is a high and dry lot with services in place, frequent it. Frequent the fuck out of it, that's a rolling terrain one mile distant. That's my heart for a grouse, that's my wingshot. That's Canada on the other side, that's where you go when you're a coward. *O the villagers are the neighbors, the villagers are the neighbors...* At present, a boat or a float plane. This will become charred in the century.

---

projected word count: 90
actual word count: 120

4

To speak your secret, a fist retracting from drywall: It's a sucking sound. To invoke as secret, replace fist. To catalogue the occasion, mix at high speed. Bake at high heat, let cool: Devour yourself in ceaseless flow. To accumulate power, the beauty of inflection. I do not know which to prefer, an icicle or barbaric glass.

---

projected word count: 70
actual word count: 57

5

You will be accused of directing the universe, of
London Bridge or misdirection. Take your cranium
at high heat until smoking, there's no retribution
here, nothing to be done, there's no smoking.

---

projected word count: 110
actual word count: 32

6

You are not for consideration, you have not
made your payments. You are frequently without
premium, an effective date of enclosure. Did you
know that in some gymnasiums there are severe
penalties for lack of responsibility? As such, I am
lowered. What is your operating margin out there,
say in weakness? I have lived a long life on procure-
ment, an ancient fleet and recent months. This is
the defense segment lagging. This is grounded
until repaired, an initial need for demand. Fiscal
2007 will be sweltering, there will be little water.

---

projected word count: 75
actual word count: 91

7

This is a complaint and a summons and a registration all at once. Take heed, she's a Vicadin question. I am willing to be neighborly here, the son of some slain. It's a human right ensured by just postage. Yes, and a group offering, and a homeless life for such soldiers. I am tranquil, and passing. I loved you as I loved nobody, and have little idea what this means. Have I loved you, or has there been nobody to love? Are you frequented, but you will not get me in court. This is vagrancy, but you will not find me slain?

---

projected word count: 125
actual word count: 102

8

An ailment or something, this is how he died. Weeping at television shows. This, and avoiding the common courtesy of sanity, which was permanent. For an affliction, fractured is fine. You may rename vaginal fluids aftershave. This will be considered comedy, or tragic. I speak like your father speaks, in syntax. I loathe this and love this. For instance, to say prostate, as in "to the doldrums," or "raped." This is not syntax, what is syntax? I cannot remember things I once read. Your father had quietly become the above-named, beside Defendant. Somebody threw a key party and everyone went home with a tumor and a vehicle. This was considered lifting into orbit, a Ferris wheel. You slowly become a blinking ball in the atmosphere, and then slowly return.

---

projected word count: 125
actual word count: 129

9

Parable: Parable. You see how this works? In my grandmother's house there were chickens, and you see, not so interesting. If you stop typing for ten minutes your monitor becomes an ocean. You forget you were typing and it all makes sense again. Sometimes you become happy, and blonde. Sometimes I thank you God for this most amazing attire, this blood suit. Frogs are croaking and the streetlamps glow. This is my father's night of working, do you know him? As transpierced, he was much like yours. As assembled, he was nothing. He had a back, to be certain: Reverse-grip pulldowns. He had a rotator cuff injury which accumulated genius. He had a happiness injury which acquired prescriptions. It was a shakedown. He told me, "Go into the universe and make loneliness, make more loneliness, Son." This as diffractive, a verb. There was a service fee assessed on all returned checks. My father as X under pending. You are over 90 days, a closing date will appear. This as a statement of your account, "Go into the universe and make gabardine, Son. Make more gabardine."

projected word count: 150
actual word count: 186

I was in love with my liver for a while, this was children to me, the difference between water and energy. A balance, I'm saying. But as your father was willing, I too invoked sacrifice. It had been deliberated by moonlight. A standard or what-not, something like Lose. This was invocation to me, a strategized. This was the cumulative effect of a liaison spent culminating. This was fornicating. There was privacy, and in some states was not. There are all-costly lessons to be learned, a money order or visit. You are required by law to report all violations, effective immediately.

---

projected word count: 165
actual word count: 100

We are neutralized, we're reflection and gone. A televised. A hydrogen jewbox. There is something to be said and you will notice infraction. He has loved you, but has loved another more so at times. This is how you were born, as static between poles. A window to a window, that's her. That's the fucking bitch you were culled away for. Excuse me.

---

projected word count: 165
actual word count: 62

I have never had dreams and have paid less for
this. As beneficiaries, you would double your odds
somewhere taxable. I am told Florida is nice. The
countess has perished by now, and I too have
inherited nothing. It has been distributed evenly,
a zero where my heart has been, O for a mouth.
Sometimes I use my telescope to look out across the
black waves at night. I see New York, I see bodies
catching fire, leaping from the penthouse rooftops.
Once I saw Hart Crane with a bottle of whiskey,
this was in a dream I did not have. He dove from
the bridge, a broker like your father. He was on
fire, and on commission. This can be considered
speculation again, but as a rule he was simplified.
I saw a gout-ridden pig named Jim Harrison. He
was eating lamb chops in the park. I entered this
into my book, and submitted the record. This was
a culling of sorts. Sometimes there are children
missing, and with my telescope I have found them.
They are in Mexico, eating beef heart stew. It's a
broth full of zeros. I tell nobody, and this can be
considered capital gain. Sometimes a child will
engage the sun with a compass or mirror, and flash
it in my direction. I put away my scope and hide. I
draw the curtains. I try not to sleep.

---

projected word count: 165
actual word count: 234

13

Try living this life with your secrets, say drinking.
For others, say capital, your dreams are in escrow.
Things are tied up around here. Your breasts and
your penises will swell up around you, this will
mean mortgages. You may dance in any corner you
wish, you mean balance. You mean write yourself
a check and don't cash it, as infinity. Place a spoon
on your nose, this is tricky, you are waiting for
friends in a bar, you will lose them. This as fore-
closure, you have not made your payments.

---

projected word count: 165
actual word count: 91

You are accruing as infidel, this is timeline. You have come from somewhere distant and have been appraised, and some thorazine. You are glutamine, and swelling. You want something. You want something compound, I can feel it.

---

projected word count: 165
actual word count: 37

Strippers aren't people, they're prophecy. You are not drunk, you are hypoglycemic. You are moccasins and a thong. Every time somebody uses ketchup I get a quarter. Coca-Cola's second-half results will be less than projected, you are less than projection. Weather has also affected this business, say in many markets with little rain.

---

projected word count: 165
actual word count: 53

Dear children, your father had continued to
sign contracts at a rapid pace. His cash assets
were receivable. This was command, as control.
Something like appearance, as position at first. He
did love you, of course, but this was on specula-
tion. There was a board of directors who rejected
his bid. During the first quarter, an inventory was
required. He spent a lot of time at the movies. He
withdrew. He purchased a well-known planet for
$42 a share in cash. This was propulsion. Things
should fall, and be complemented, and cooled, was
his motto. I watched your father write those letters,
and kiss them, and fold them into periods. His was
a niche market, and the countess became relative.
Ammunition sales remained steady. He dipped his
poems, he set them on fire. This was an expensive
first quarter. There was seasonal fall-off. We were
operating on credit costs and a nickel per sheet.
This was cosmic attraction, and entry.

---

projected word count: 165
actual word count: 160

This was operation. Approximately 84% of his revenue was from longing. In the company's view, well positioned for stalling.

---

projected word count: 50
actual word count: 20

Mine was a family of four zoned commercial. My father had entered the universe on a phallus, riding it through the sea. He splintered us with his prodding. This was integral, and became dividends. I wished he had loved me as a long-term prospect. When I met your own father he was a medical error without focus. The north and south poles as infrastructure, I'm saying. Your father was two things at once, as was mine. The countess was pleased. I retreated for a while, and was relegated to garnishing. This was longitude and lassitude, stretched out and weak. There was a point where the ecliptic became intersection, and a backlog was identified. I loved you for a moment as I loved myself as the child of my father, as children to be loved not for fuck's sake but healthcare. This can be considered initiative and issuance. This is something like buffer, and belief. This was postmodern, and strikingly venereal.

---

projected word count: 120
actual word count: 160

OUR FATHER IN THE ATMOSPHERE

as response

Exosphere

After all these years our father has remained in the normal style. I think: Definition, and he becomes "character". There's something of a larger audience in this. To wit: My brother, as music hall comedian, may wax himself into a corner, perceptive of plot. There is communal pleasure to be had in the form of chocolate, or religious rites, but juggler? I knew a young girl who said, "That's the fish of Christ on your car." She was all body, and clean, and the car wasn't mine and the fish wasn't Christ's. It was a sticker made in Taiwan where fish were becoming hugely popular as food. I do not believe that Christ would have opinions, and this is what has made it so difficult to care for my brother. We never drove, we took the trains, and there were years when I would carry him in my arms like a burrowing, mile after mile into what was perceived as the moral universe. This was forward and always faster. Not as wisdom, but attitude. I allowed myself to suffer for it, and am suffering still for this allowance. Yep, but not my brother. Not my object who in those moments wrapped his limbs and clung to life, who rode my body into a parallel venture, seeking form over phantom as opposed to what's verse.

Exosphere

Was our father sensuous in his compensation, or was this a comic mask, say in the matter of the countess or drafted scenes? Who was she to have ruled him over else if not a master of disgust? As I told my brother, may she burn in Hell or partisanship, but that's a lukewarm calculus. I am only graceless/ at the slight of wit/ at the cannot before the alter/ am graced/ by fluids of / the concentrated image. This as return, which you have written to us of. Please take into consideration some fantasia, one deserves a new name over provincialism. Having spent all my time in the company of a child, I am more likely lead than levity in this.

Exosphere

I am concerned with one meaning in one context. For instance, my father on an island. This means he was destitute, and under situations preemptive. One strikes out toward love. If despair, that much further. This can be witnessed in the form of a countess. Or symphony. I will allow myself the dream of a broken-down car and my father as hostile toward witnesses. This can be considered truth, and standard for prejudice in any language but greatness. My father as hostility: Is this not destitute as well? If so, then I have no answer as to why he sought love in one instance, while literature in ours. Why the supernatural pitted against norm? O our father, king of the universe, I command you to awaken from this half-burned barn.

Exosphere

On Judge Joe Brown this afternoon there was a woman suing her
husband for degenerative bowel disease. I ate potato chips, and
watched her say, "He done it to me after being with that waitress,
and now I poop all the time, or I cain't poop at all. Is my bowels,
Your Honor." This was in the amount of $1,700. Tonight I'll dance,
I think, and hold my brother close, like a baby again. I hope he
falls asleep. I hope that in heaven there's a word for something
like heaven, that it doesn't end there. I can't bear to think of my
brother as having nowhere left to go, as being written somehow.
In audit, what's on the page is falsely flourished. I'll send my
brother skyward, not as search for flight but flight. What's true
or not's a signaling. My brother as passage, what's left behind as
finally calm.

Exosphere

When we were children our father began a scaffolding, as opposition. This was planks and nails, and inner order. My class was listless apathy, and being babe, my brother slept and called this Soul. I might have desired mental mores if not for hope. What did I know, what did I know of love's austere and lonely orifice: Our father as desire, or building toward. My brother as dreaming, and dream as joy, or permanence, or levity. The hole becomes my ambition now, as vagrancy in the matter of attendance. I am ordered to reform the synonym here. That's our father speaking, in the broadband sense. What's out there is nuts and bolts somehow: Come in Supernova, Come in.

Exosphere

My brother has asked that I speak of his documents. He has tugged my sleeve, but well equipped as witness there's a syntax in what's non. On paper he's been crude of class, on stone or stage a miracle. I may make my meaning clearer by a simple instance, but why. If this is but for help alone then help's a snare. Your generation has rendered service without sufficiency, mine's for what's as bad. My brother's of a different arm, alight for what's beyond, adrift, but not as sad. Or, alternately: Here are my brother's stones, polished after a century of plugging them in. Here is my brother as seller of stones: "Would you like to buy some stones?" A smile on his face. An infinite holding in his eyes, flickering bright. I want to walk out into the ocean and drown in the undertow, moor to the floor. He's so beautiful I want to cry.

Exosphere

You are the accumulation of our father's sins. You are in a position, anyway, and as clouds position themselves over the tumbling earth so too have you positioned your object. Or clouds before the earth, or you before our father, or he before us. As there were stars positioned upon our ceiling: they glowed in the dark, and as I kept my brother warm in bed above our beams were stars aglow as well. And beyond them worlds, and within those worlds were other stars. And beyond those stars were other worlds, and within those worlds were photographs. This was dreaming. This was not to be outdone by waking. This was to be considered prophecy, that in dreams we'd lift our arms to the universe and watch our father spiral away: as blinking lights in the atmosphere, as something extra, and terrestrial, and guided toward heaven?

Exosphere

On Judge Joe Brown today, there was a man who wanted his bamboo steamer back. He was considered the plaintiff, and his girlfriend was counter-suing for lack of affection in the amount of $6,000. Once I dyed my hair to match my computer. Is this the same? My favorite time of year became those weeks when my roots were growing in. This was constant, and I often wondered if suffering were simply the lack of pain. I was always happy, and on the verge of something awful. I used to make up limericks for my brother: When he was sad, I would sing, "I have woken each Autumn to the sound of leaves, in Winter to the sound of none, in Spring I have woken to the sound of rain, in Summer to the sound of sun." I would lull him to sleep. Sometimes I would watch the television, sometimes I would think: Is lack of affection the absence of limericks? No I wouldn't.

Exosphere

To think that some people express themselves over dinner–this is difficult, to be fresh, and permanently valuable. Here you have come to our help, but one must suspend one's belief. I have accompanied poetry, or this was throwing light upon each other. I am as much shocked as taken to be trouble. Hyperbolically one might say public occasion, and mean a mass vomiting. The author of this work has been affected by representation. These are your definitive options: Yes. Or, alternately: No.

Exosphere

Once I saw my brother levitating and he screamed, "Look, Sis,
I'm crisscross applesauce!" I cried, and held myself (as a record
of impression) but this was temporary. My brother as elevation,
something like an exhibit for bananas, and persistence. Is this
joy? I have been following an aesthetic, not insanity. Once when
I expected language to approach maturity I grew breasts. There
was no turning back for me then, the eminent became frailty. This
was in the stars, I believe. Ten-thousand Asian Minors bisected in
the sky as cryptogram want me to believe in obscurity. There are
people suffering for godsake, but I am by no means convinced
that a poem like *Anabase* requires a preface. Between order and
chaos, one is discussion.

Exosphere

But back to my brother: It's not easy raising a young boy as distinction. There is immediate meaning in wealth, or recitation. What's in this century? Tomorrow on Judge Joe Brown our father's ghost will appear, or he will appear as himself from the greater misgivings. What will he say? Will he look me in my eyes, I wonder, across the frequency of this, our "object"—My brother says: "I hope he speaks in Spanish—That would be cool!" I am waiting to become occupied.

Exosphere

I find it so strange that our father would shave himself. Was this amusement, or a living? I am only now sexual, though I have selected prose to hint otherwise. My favorite position is intention: Though hard to come by, a craft nonetheless. On television there are tribesmen who create a broth by soaking their own testicles in rain water. This is considered the opposite of impotency, circa BC. You can imagine they are pinkish and swollen between their legs. Is this what it means to have interests? I wanted to believe that the emptiness supplied connection, a vortex within which we spun as random variables reaching toward deeper, darker space. A system of ethics, or ill health. It is my responsibility now to sermon and impulse, to make verbs out of pretense. Inevitably. I am tempted to lather my body tonight, and draw up the blade. What's behind it is space, but it will grow back with language?

Exosphere

Your letters found us well and in passage. The beginning of the
second act was weakness, but that's a prodigal urge. To estab-
lish a pattern is to beg its interruption. For instance, one might
say: Martin does not love me, Martin won't call. Martin calls Eric,
Martin won't call. Cathy is lovely, Martin won't call—the desired
effect is like shrubbery: you're in it outside the window. As a
dramatist, fisticuffs. Ad absurdity, producer and cast. Sea's the
weather in Baltimore, a bewildered minute lasting forever: One
evidence of this is the appearance of ill-fated figures. Take the
combatants, for example. The living. Dressed as dead, we're face-
down in a green bog together, waiting for orbit.

Exosphere

Dear Sir, I am accounted for. What's diminishing is sacrifice, the manner of a doctrine or atom before God. The supply of our time is in bulk or as victory. I believe a step toward making the modern world possible is bereavement: A footnote continues the reader, but as guilt over evidence. On Judge Joe Brown this week the bailiff rolled in a fat woman on a silver gurney and announced her as Defendant. She was placed at center court, and measured out as enormous. The following was an eerie silence: It began as a swaying among the pews. It ended as a swaying among the pews.